How to Draw Christmas

Amit Offir

www.amitoffir.com

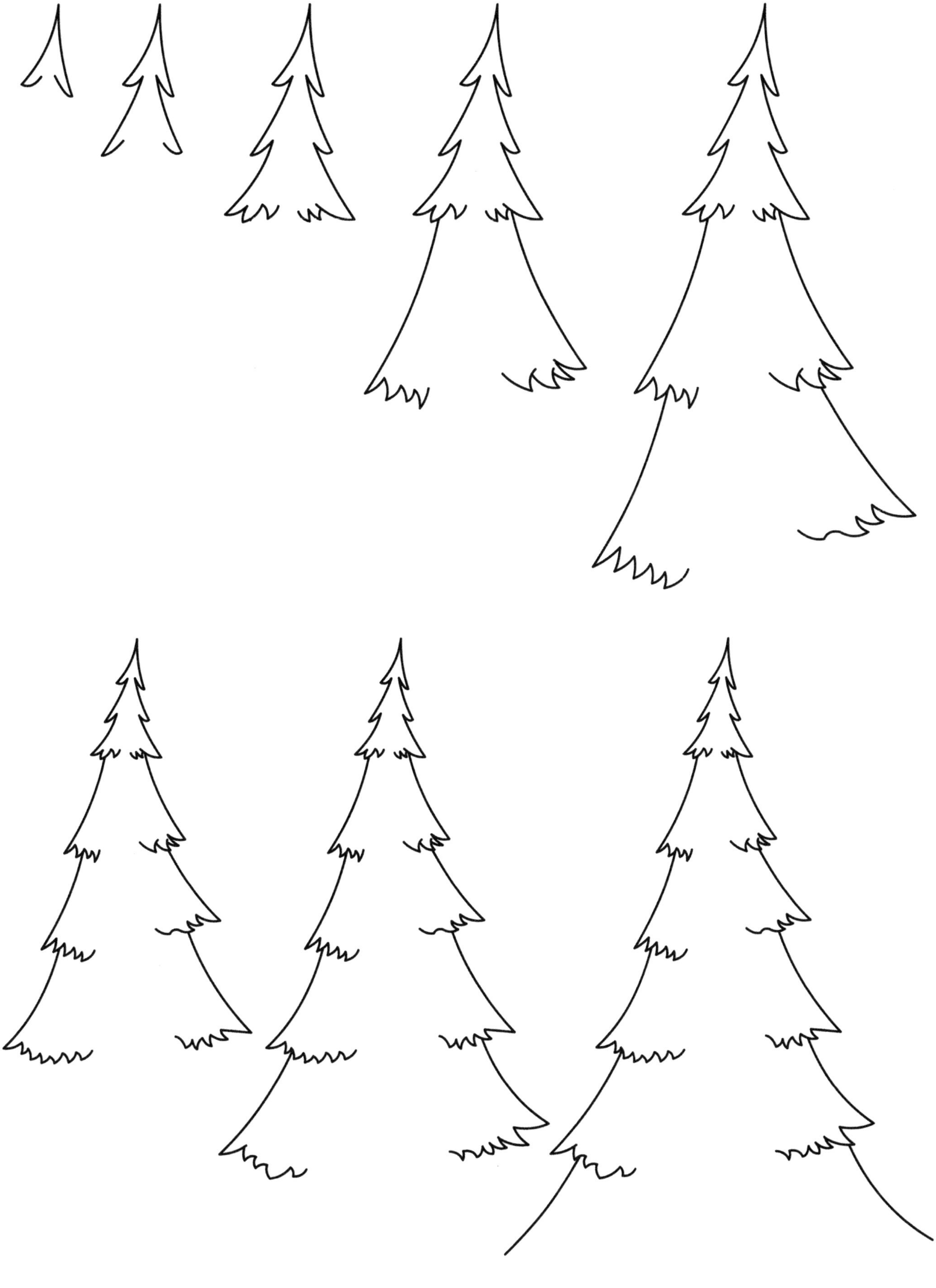

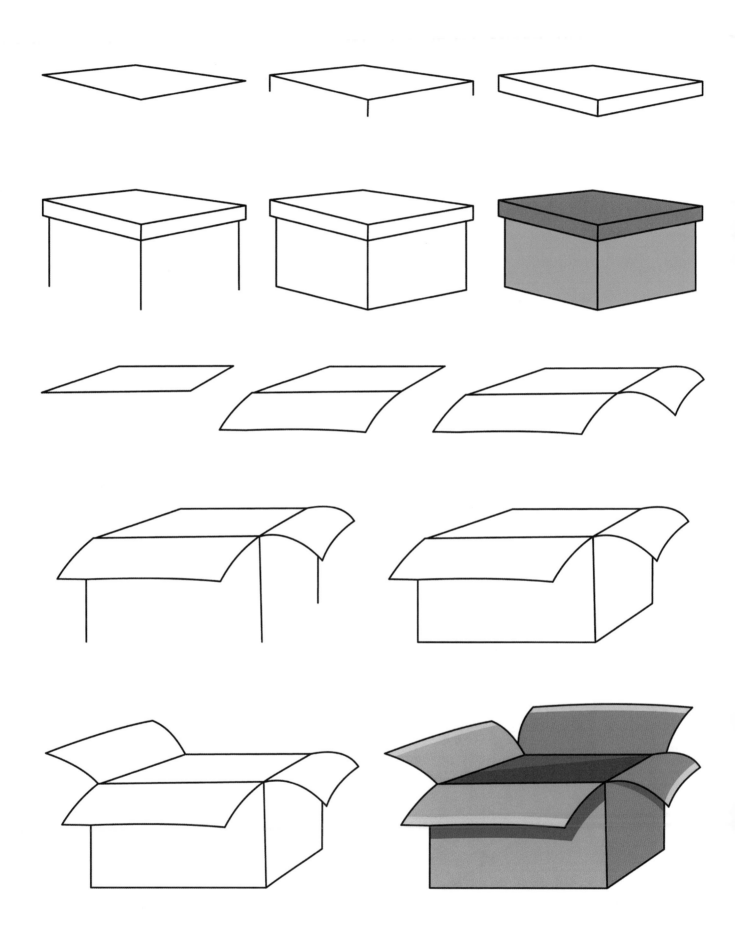

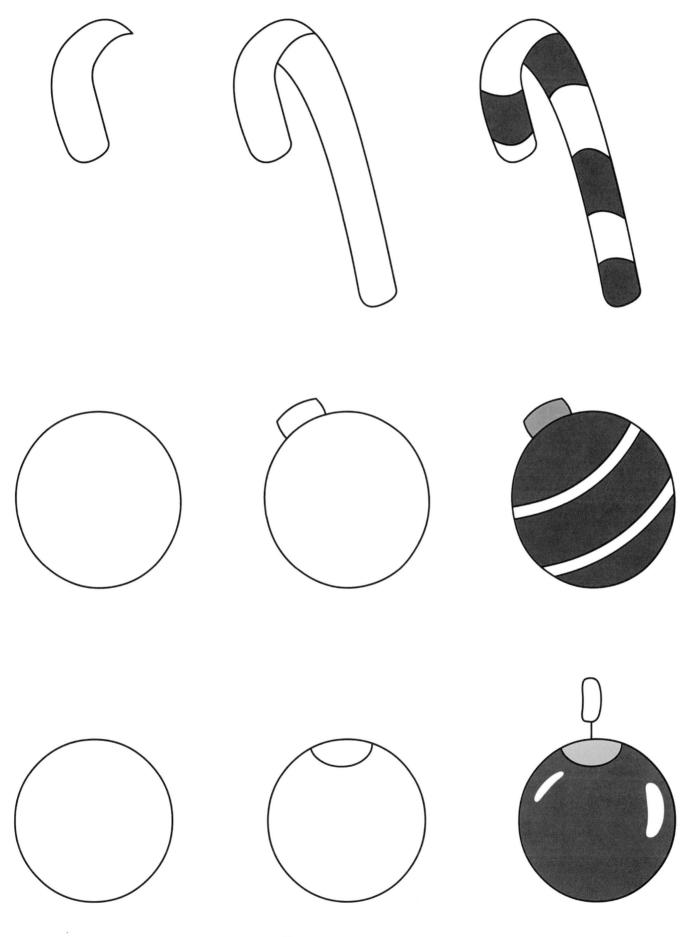

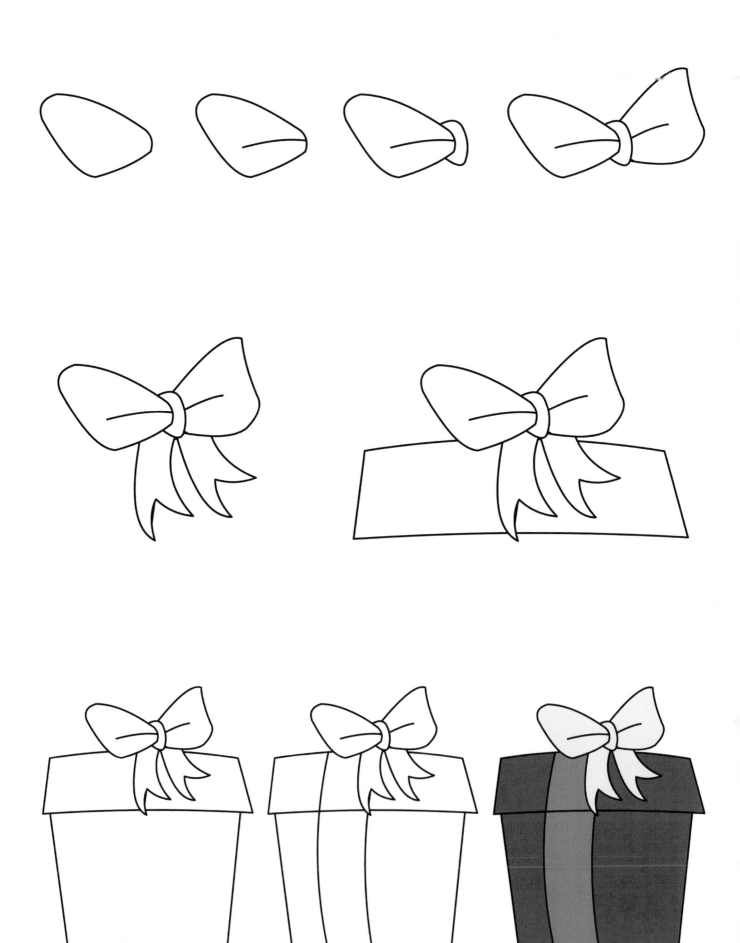

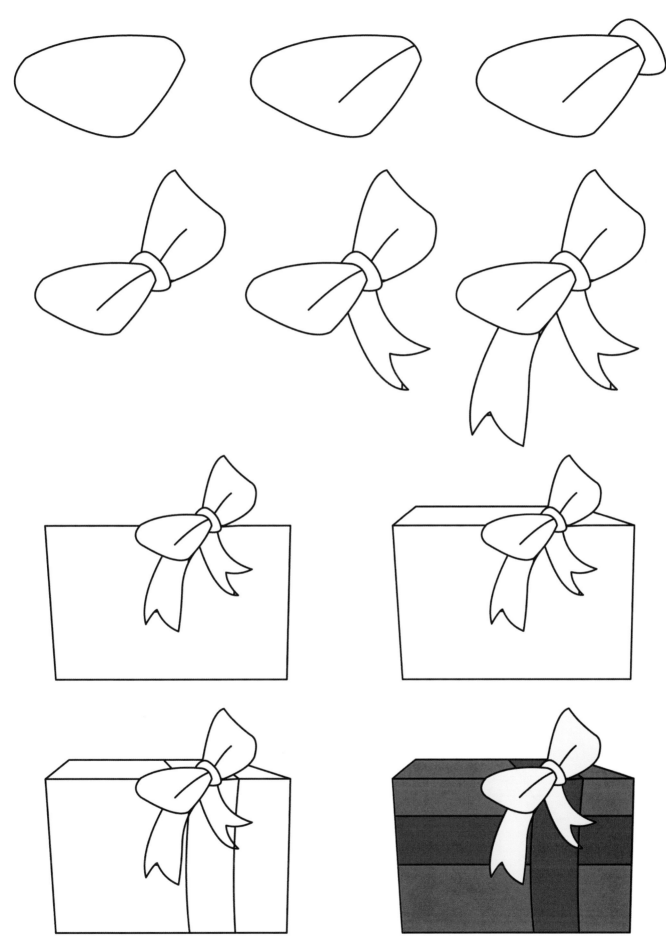

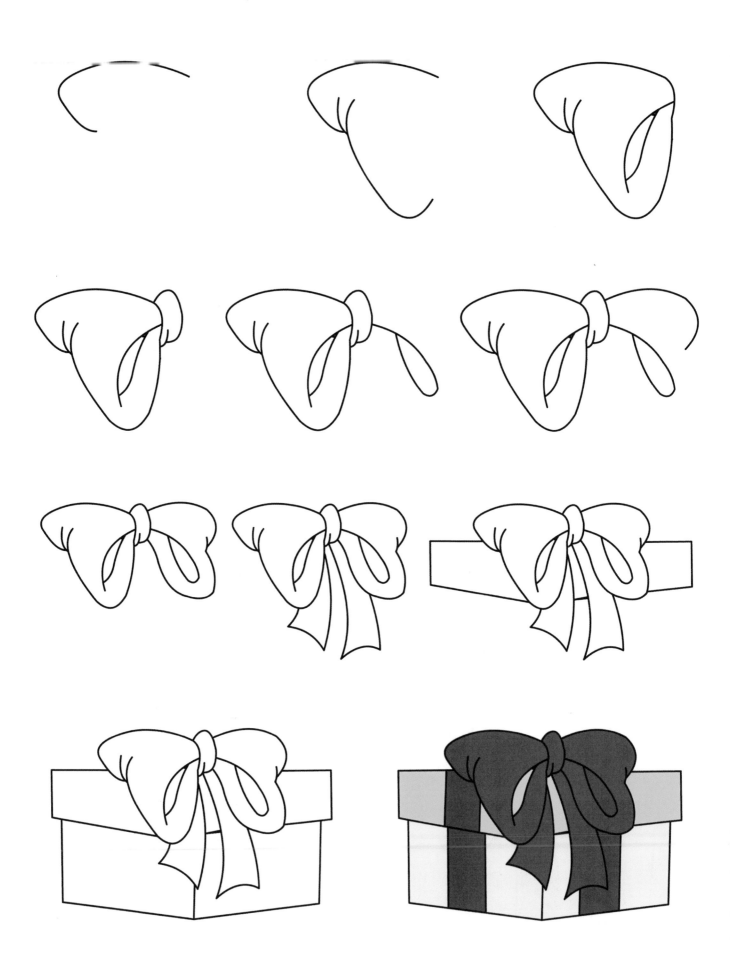

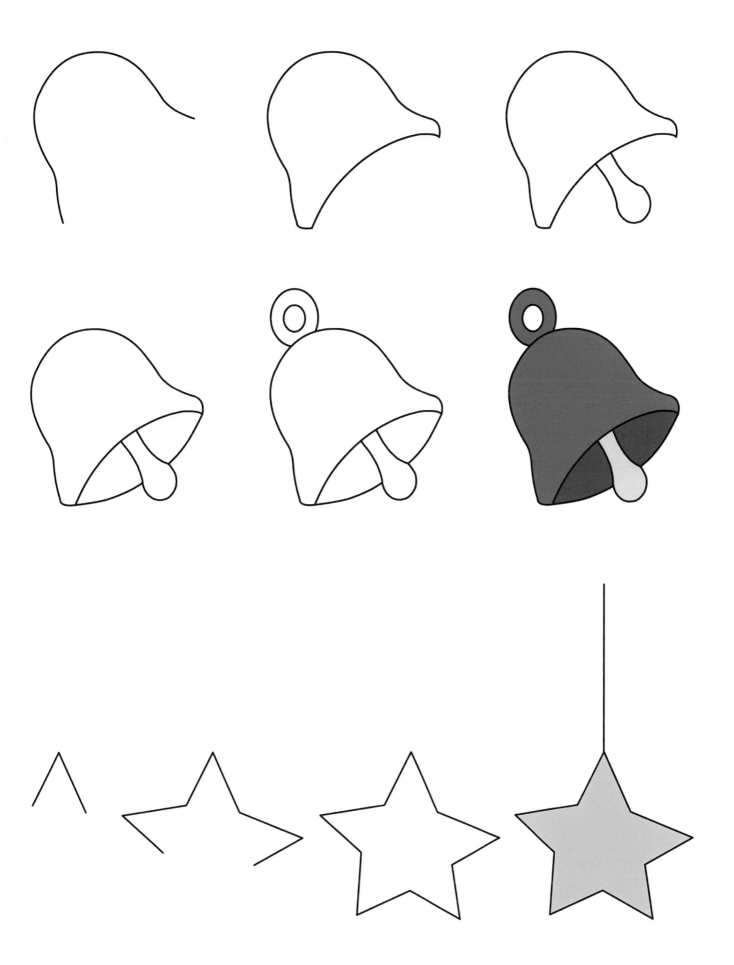

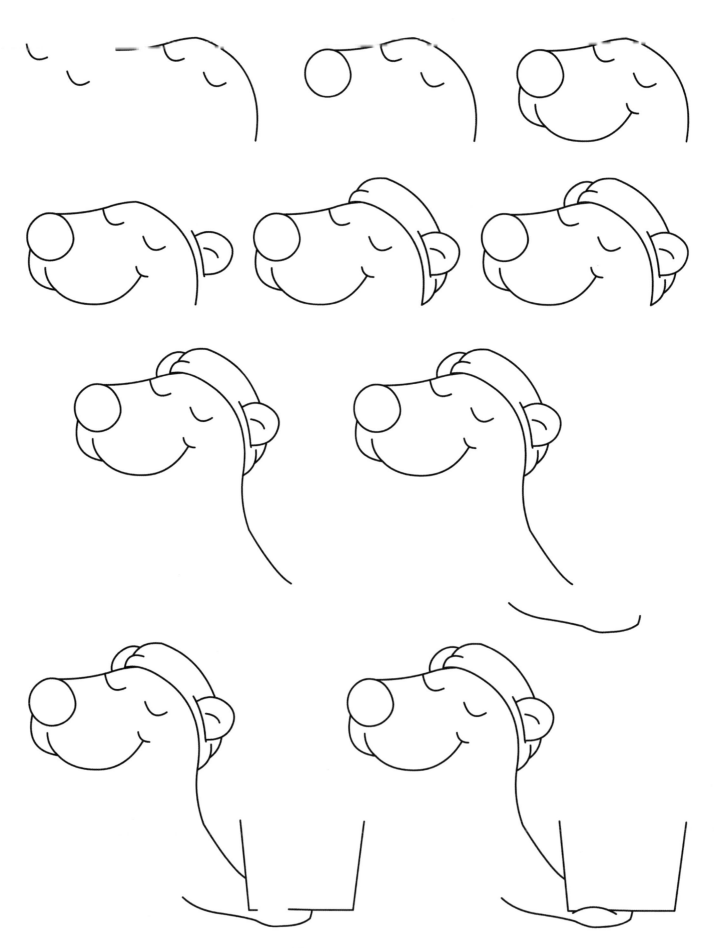

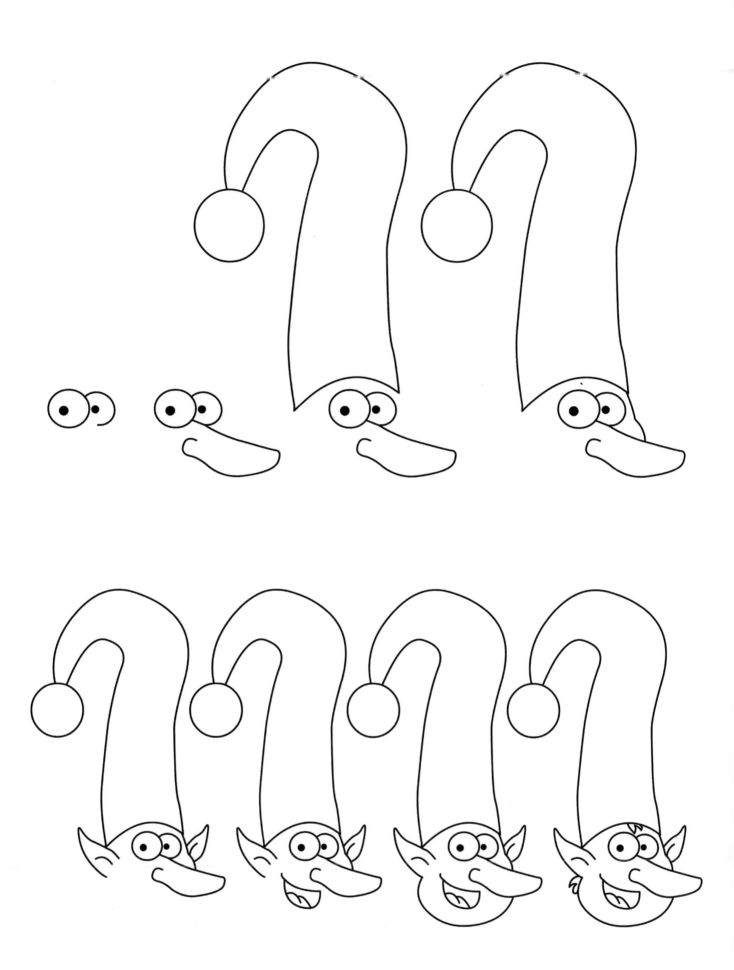

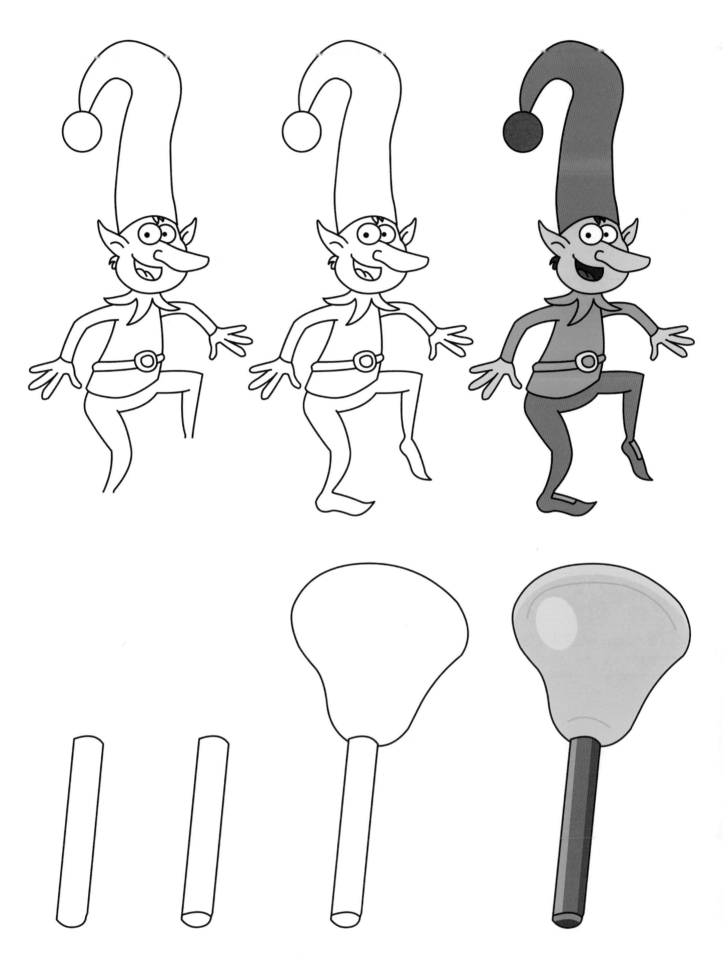

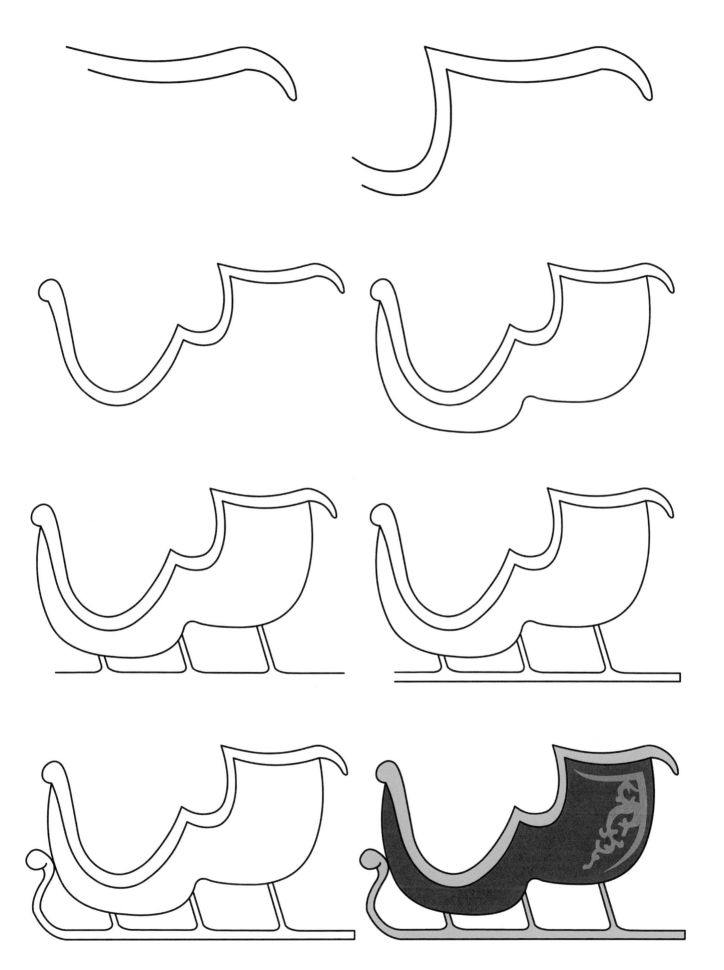

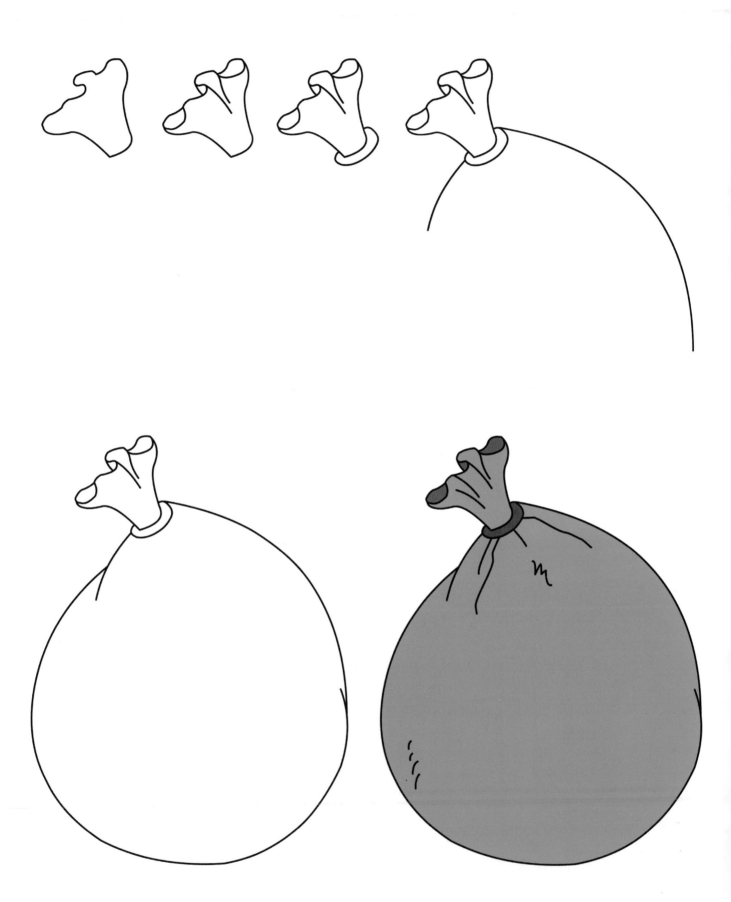

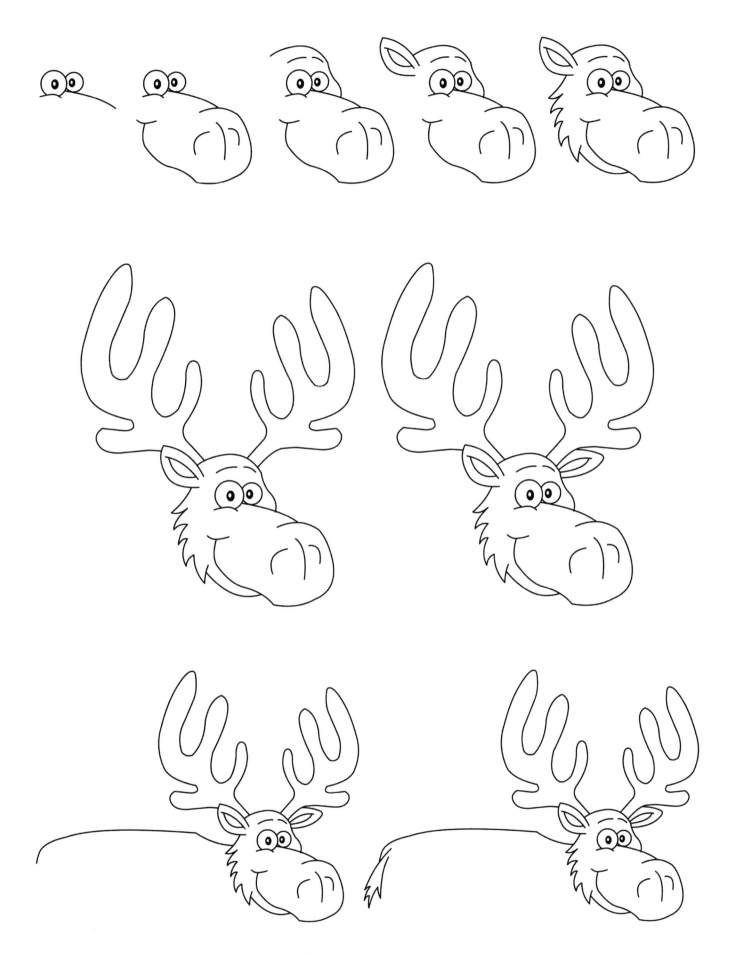

About The Author

Amit Offir is a renowned illustrator, author, and comics artist.

His first book "The Beetle That Wants To Be" is one of his bestsellers.

On the year 2005 he developed a uniqe technique for drawing

comics and cartoon characters in a few easy steps.

He named it "Drawing Easily".

This technique was invented after drawing over 500,000 drawings

on stones.

Amit lectures and teaches comics lessons and meets thousands

of children and adults every year around the world.

You are welcome to get farther information about Amit Offir's art,

licensing and more, in the "Troubadour" official website

www.troubadour.co.il

Enjoy this series of books and keep on drawing!

Best regards.

Books in this series

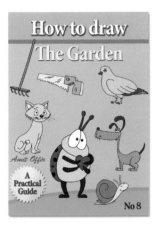

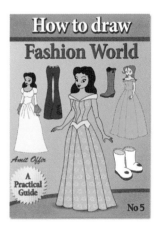

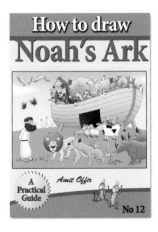

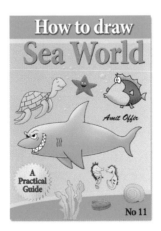

And many more!

Enter the official website - www.troubadour.co.il

4962015R00022

Printed in Great Britain
by Amazon.co.uk, Ltd.,
Marston Gate.